THE KOMODO DRAGON

BY LISA OWINGS

BELLWETHER MEDIA • MINNEAPOLIS, MN

Jump into the cockpit and take flight with
Pilot Books. Your journey will take you on
high-energy adventures as you learn about
all that is wild, weird, fascinating, and fun!

This edition first published in 2012 by Bellwether Media, Inc.

No part of this publication may be reproduced in whole or in part without written permission of the publisher.
For information regarding permission, write to Bellwether Media, Inc., Attention: Permissions Department,
5357 Penn Avenue South, Minneapolis, MN 55419.

Library of Congress Cataloging-in-Publication Data

Owings, Lisa.
 The Komodo dragon / by Lisa Owings.
   p. cm. – (Pilot books. Nature's deadliest)
 Includes bibliographical references and index.
 Summary: "Fascinating images accompany information about the Komodo dragon. The combination of high-interest
subject matter and narrative text is intended for students in grades 3 through 7"–Provided by publisher.
 ISBN 978-1-60014-667-1 (hardcover : alk. paper)
 1. Komodo dragon–Juvenile literature. I. Title.
 QL666.L29O95 2012
 597.95'968–dc22   2011013765

Printed in the United States of America, North Mankato, MN.

080111   1187

CONTENTS

Park ranger Main had spent 25 years working with Komodo dragons in Komodo National Park, Indonesia. As he worked in his hut, he started thinking about the change in their behavior. Komodo dragons never used to attack humans, but reports of injuries and deaths had begun to pile up. The dragons had become more aggressive after the rangers stopped feeding them. It used to be common for rangers to feed the dragons dead goats. This attracted large numbers of the lizards for study and kept them away from humans on the island.

Just two years before, a Komodo dragon had killed an 8-year-old boy who was fishing with his uncle. Main was glad that his hut rested on stilts above the ground. The dragons would never be able to climb all the way up. Or so he thought.

Main heard a faint noise on the stairs to his hut. He continued with his work, expecting a knock on the door. Instead, he felt razor-sharp teeth sink into his ankle. A Komodo dragon had climbed the stairs and crept under his desk! He could feel the dragon trying to tear his flesh from his bone. Main reached under the desk and tried to pry the deadly jaws off his leg. The dragon let go of his ankle only to sink its teeth into Main's hand. Main screamed. He fought with the dragon and hoped someone would hear his cries for help. His friends arrived quickly. They used large sticks to drive the dragon away.

Tree Houses

Young Komodo dragons live in trees until they are too large to jump from branch to branch.

The Delicious Dead

Komodo dragons have been known to dig up human remains from graves and feast on the decaying flesh.

Main's friends saw that he was badly injured. His ankle and hand were shredded and dripping with both blood and the Komodo dragon's saliva. They had to get him to the hospital, but the nearest one was on a different island. The men piled into a boat and sped to the island of Bali. Main's hand and ankle were extremely swollen when they got there. He was nearly unconscious. The doctors rushed to give him antibiotics to fight the infection.

After the Attack

Main needed more than 50 stitches to close his wounds. His hand was still swollen three months later, but he had survived the brutal attack. Main would never let the deadly Komodo dragon catch him off guard again.

Deadly Lizard

The Komodo dragon is the largest lizard in the world. Its giant size and deadly reputation have made it legendary in many parts of the world. However, the Komodo dragon lives on only a few small islands in Indonesia. The dragon is a monitor, a type of lizard that has been around for more than 250 million years. Most monitors are small. However, Komodo dragons have grown large because they have few predators. They can be 10 feet (3 meters) long and weigh around 300 pounds (135 kilograms). Deer and wild boars are their favorite prey, but they can take down animals as large as water buffalo. A water buffalo can weigh eight times more than a Komodo dragon!

Komodo dragon   **human**

Indonesia

N
W • E
S

Komodo

Flores

Rinca

Komodo dragon territory = ▢

Australia

Diving Dragons

Komodo dragons can swim at a depth of about 20 feet (6 meters) for 300 feet (91 meters) before coming up for air. Their powerful tails swish back and forth to push them through the water. This is how Komodo dragons ended up on several Indonesian islands.

A Komodo dragon's jaws can be even more terrifying than its size. It has sharp, serrated teeth that curve toward the back of its mouth. This shape is perfect for tearing large chunks of flesh from unlucky victims. Even more horrifying, the mouth of a Komodo dragon is full of deadly bacteria. Victims of dragon bites almost never escape without a life-threatening infection.

A Komodo dragon also produces venom in glands along its lower jaw. The venom oozes between the dragon's teeth as it bites. This poison causes prey to bleed to death quickly and become too weak to fight back. The dragon can devour prey in minutes. It sinks its teeth in and shakes its head back and forth to rip off huge pieces of flesh. Then it tilts its head back to swallow. The dragon's jaws separate so it can swallow smaller animals whole.

Megalania

Megalania is an ancient relative of the Komodo dragon. It lived over 40,000 years ago. This giant lizard is thought to be the largest poisonous animal that ever lived. It grew to be more than 23 feet (7 meters) long and weighed around 1,300 pounds (600 kilograms).

A Little Help

When trying to swallow an animal whole, Komodo dragons have been known to hammer it down their throats by pushing against the trunks of trees.

Chill Out

Komodo dragons are cold-blooded animals. They bathe in the sun to heat their bodies and move into the shade to cool off. After feeding, dragons seek shade so they can digest their food before it rots inside their stomachs.

Komodo dragons spend most of the day on the hunt. They can run up to 11 miles (18 kilometers) per hour in short bursts. This is fast enough to catch many small animals. In order to catch larger, faster prey, the Komodo dragon must hide and wait. It flicks its forked tongue around to smell and taste the air for signs of approaching prey. The dragon senses a deer nearby. It charges at the deer with its deadly mouth open. The deer gets away, but not without a gaping wound. The dragon knows the deer will soon die from poisoning or infection. Such a tasty meal will be worth the wait.

Komodo dragons live alone from birth. Their deadliest predators are other Komodo dragons. Adult dragons often eat eggs, young dragons, or even smaller adult dragons. They are careful to avoid each other. However, adult dragons will come together to feast if they smell the rotting flesh of a dead animal. They can smell carrion up to 7 miles (11 kilometers) away. They flick their tongues in and out to find the kill. The largest dragons are the first to sink their teeth in. When smaller dragons arrive, they are careful not to get in the way. They sneak a few mouthfuls here and there while the large dragons stuff themselves until their bellies touch the ground.

Stuffed!
Komodo dragons can eat almost their entire weight in one meal.

Komodo dragons rarely attack humans, but when they do, the attacks are often lethal. Most attacks occur because a dragon feels threatened. Many people travel to Indonesia to see the dragons in person. Sometimes they get too close. If a person corners a Komodo dragon, the lizard will open its mouth and hiss loudly. It will lift and curl its powerful tail, preparing to strike. If the person does not back away, the dragon will charge.

Komodo dragons also attack humans who look like easy prey. A dragon will attack someone who appears to be injured. If a person falls or is lying on the ground, he or she is vulnerable to a Komodo dragon attack. Young children are also tempting targets because of their small size and fearlessness.

Attack Facts

- Since Komodo dragons were discovered in the 1900s, records show fewer than 20 attacks on humans.

- Only five deaths have been confirmed from Komodo dragon attacks since 1974. Four of these deaths have occurred since 2000.

Back from the Dead

Some peoples native to islands of Indonesia believe that Komodo dragons hold the spirits of their dead relatives. Natives often sacrifice goats and other animals to the dragons.

Komodo dragon attacks can be prevented. People on tours should listen to their guides and never wander from their group. They should stay quiet and give the dragons space. Most tour guides carry a forked stick to keep dragons from coming within charging distance.

Many zoos across the country give visitors the opportunity to safely observe and learn about Komodo dragons without traveling to Indonesia. Learning more about these ancient lizards will help us protect them and their island homes. It will also help us better understand their behavior and how to avoid the poisonous jaws of these deadly dragons.

Glossary

antibiotics—drugs used to kill bacteria

bacteria—very small organisms; bacteria can be helpful or harmful to humans.

carrion—dead and decaying flesh

glands—organs that produce natural chemicals

infection—an illness caused by harmful bacteria; Komodo dragon saliva has bacteria in it that can cause infections.

lethal—deadly

monitor—a kind of lizard that eats mostly meat and has a forked tongue; monitors are most common in tropical areas of Africa, Asia, and Australia.

saliva—spit; this watery fluid helps animals swallow food.

serrated—having jagged edges; Komodo dragon teeth are serrated.

stilts—tall posts that hold a home or building above the ground

unconscious—not awake or aware

venom—poison that some animals produce and use to kill other animals

vulnerable—in a position of being easily hurt

To Learn More

At the Library

Belknap, Jodi Parry, and Tamara Montgomery. *Kraken-ka the Komodo Dragon: A Tale of Indonesia*. Honolulu, HI: Calabash Books, 2007.

Crump, Martha. *Mysteries of the Komodo Dragon: The Biggest, Deadliest Lizard Gives Up Its Secrets*. Honesdale, Pa.: Boyds Mills Press, 2010.

Lutz, Dick, and J. Marie Lutz. *Komodo: The Living Dragon*. Salem, Ore.: Dimi Press, 1997.

On the Web

Learning more about Komodo dragons is as easy as 1, 2, 3.

1. Go to www.factsurfer.com.

2. Enter "Komodo dragons" into the search box.

3. Click the "Surf" button and you will see a list of related Web sites.

With factsurfer.com, finding more information is just a click away.

Index